72-502

D0871286

7 1994

5

8

Creating with BEADS

By Grethe LaCroix

LITTLE CRAFT BOOK SERIES

STERLING PUBLISHING CO., INC. **NEW YORK**
SAUNDERS OF TORONTO, Ltd., Don Mills, Canada

Oak Tree Press Co., Ltd.
Distributed by WARD LOCK, Ltd., London & Sydney

Little Craft Book Series

Beads Plus Macramé

Candle-Making

Coloring Papers

Corrugated Carton Crafting

Creating with Beads

Creating with Burlap

Felt Crafting

Macramé

Making Paper Flowers

Masks

Metal and Wire Sculpture

Model Boat Building

Nail Sculpture

Potato Printing

Repoussage

Scissorscraft

Sewing without a Pattern

Whittling and Wood Carving

Drawings by Robert Metz
Photographs by Joost Guntenaar
Translated by Eric Greweldinger

Fourth Printing, 1971
Copyright © 1969 by
Sterling Publishing Co., Inc.
419 Park Avenue South, New York, N.Y. 10016
Simultaneously Published and Copyright © 1969 in Canada
by Saunders of Toronto, Ltd., Don Mills, Ontario
British edition published by Oak Tree Press Co., Ltd.
Distributed in Great Britain and the Commonwealth by
Ward Lock, Ltd., 116 Baker Street, London W1
The original edition was published in the Netherlands under the
title "Kralen" © 1967 by Cantecleer De Bilt, De Bilt, Netherlands.
Manufactured in the United States of America
All rights reserved
Library of Congress Catalog Card No.: 69-19487
ISBN 0–8069–5124–9   UK 7061 2169 4
5125 –7

Contents

Before You Begin

Beadcraft—stringing beads, or embroidering or weaving with beads—is creative work. Whoever does it is bound to project his or her personality into it. It is the purpose of this book to show you how fascinating beadwork is and how to produce little beaded works of art that will give you satisfaction and pleasure.

The techniques of the craft are not in themselves difficult, but in order to master them, some attention and patience are needed at the start, as beads, especially small ones, are not always easy to handle. For their modest size, beads hold great lustre and beauty, and the effort beadcraft requires can be amply rewarded in the results attained.

Before you begin, you need some rules to guide you, not directions about the techniques to be applied—you will find these on the later pages— but some general considerations and pieces of advice, based on many years of experience. Before you start, collect all the beads you like and keep them preferably in small glass jars, so that they are fully visible. Then put a piece of felt or velvet of neutral color in front of you on a table or—better still—on a low-rimmed tray. This will prevent the beads from rolling away. Also, keep close at hand all the materials you may need, so that you will not have to interrupt your work time and again.

The rewards of beadcraft are in creating lovely, useful objects like this eardrop.

You will need a few cups for selecting the beads, some nylon thread (or nylon fishing line) and a darning needle or so to start. More on materials later. Let us first get to work on the initial project.

Necklace Made with a Looped Thread

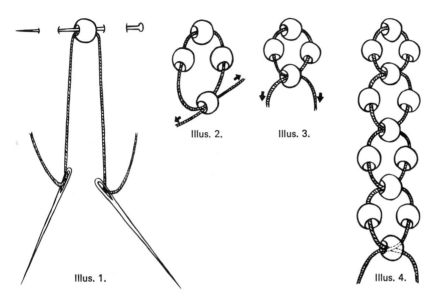

Illus. 1.

Illus. 2.

Illus. 3.

Illus. 4.

Illus. 1 to 4. These diagrams show the four steps in the basic technique of threading beads.

A single, looped thread gives two thread-ends and so its use is called the two-thread technique. This technique forms the basis of all beadwork dealt with in this book. It allows for endless variations and you can apply it not only to necklaces, but also to brooches, medallions and earrings.

The string in Illus. 4 has been made by the simplest application of the two-thread, or basic, technique. Start with a long thread, and run it through one bead. Position this bead at a point halfway down the length of the thread, and keep it in place by fixing it to a sand-filled pincushion (Illus. 1) to hold while you are doing the rest of the threading. This step forms the looped thread.

Now continue with both ends of the thread

(either with two needles—or without needles if you have used a stiff nylon fishing line). Thread one bead at the left side of the central bead and two at the right. Now cross the threads through the last-threaded bead (Illus. 2), thus connecting the four beads. Pull the two thread-ends downward (Illus. 3). Continue with three beads each time, until the desired length has been attained (Illus. 4).

Before you pull up the last bead, apply some glue to the threads. Then, after you pull the threads through, they will be fixed inside the bead and you can cut the thread-ends off. This is the basic method used to make the necklace of coral beads and glass bars shown in Illus. 5. However, you must add a clasp for opening and

Illus. 5. How to make this necklace of bars and beads is diagrammed on the next page. Medallion in the middle is dealt with in the following chapter.

closing the necklace, and this requires a slight change in threading.

Start with a glass bar as shown in Illus. 6. This bar will be part of the clasp. (In old-fashioned ornaments, the bar was made of gold or silver and was slipped through a little ring.) Take a piece of thread that is approximately four times the circumference you want the necklace to be. Run the thread through the glass bar, and position the bar halfway down the thread. Attach the bar to the pincushion. Knot the two threads together before continuing.

Proceed to thread the nine beads leading up to the second glass bar as shown in Illus. 6. After threading the second bar use the basic two-thread technique to continue. Be careful to thread so that the large beads are at the bottom of the necklace and the smaller ones are at the top, in order to make the necklace lie round.

The necklace ends with eight beads and the closing loop of the clasp (Illus. 6). Run the threads a few times in a circle through the six beads of the closing loop. You will notice in Illus. 6 that the threads are knotted together before starting the six-bead loop. To complete the project, you again apply glue to the threads before inserting them into the last bead or beads, and finally you cut the thread-ends off.

The necklace described here can also be executed with jet beads and black glass bars to go with the bracelet shown on page 23. Or you can use wooden beads of different colors combined with round or angular wooden bars. Wooden beads would be very suitable for a child's necklace, and a little girl could be kept occupied in a pleasant way by making such a necklace.

Wooden beads can also be attractively combined with beads made of glass, minerals or ceramic material. Mat-surface beads alternating with glazed ones and round beads alternating with oval or tubular ones are effective combinations. The examples in this book will give you ideas on selecting beads for your projects. Your own taste and imagination will also guide you.

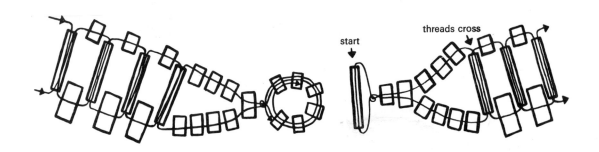

Illus. 6. At the right is the start of the necklace. Threads cross in the second bar and you continue in the basic technique. At the left is the end of the necklace with its circular closing.

Illus. 7. Medallions to be hung around the neck as pendants or made into brooches are threaded in a slightly different way, as you will see on the next pages.

Medallion Technique

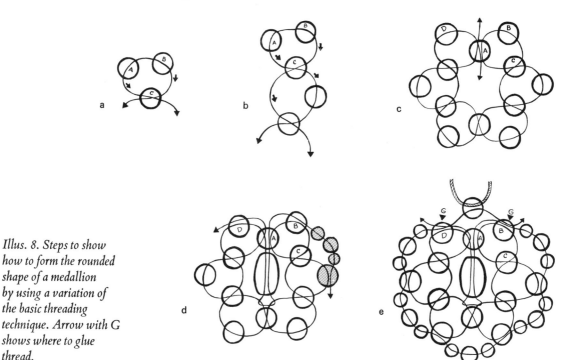

Illus. 8. Steps to show how to form the rounded shape of a medallion by using a variation of the basic threading technique. Arrow with G shows where to glue thread.

You make a medallion or pendant like the ones in Illus. 7 by the two-thread technique with a variation. Now you start with three beads instead of four, and you continue with two instead of three (Illus. 8a and 8b). In this way, the shape becomes round.

Once again, you take a long thread and start in the middle of it, as you can see in Illus. 8a.

When the string of beads fits around the large bead to be placed in the middle, the circle is closed (Illus. 8c). It is a good idea to start by first putting the loose beads around the central bead, in order to find out the quantity you will need. The pendant gets round if you put a round bead in the middle and oval if the central bead is oval.

Illus. 8c shows how you close the circle around

Bead Accessories

In some of the following projects, you will want to use metal clasps instead of a beaded loop-and-bar arrangement. There are many kinds of clasps. The type pictured here can be decorated with a medallion. Also, you can attach your medallions to metal discs and thus create a brooch. To jewellers, these metal accessories are known as "findings," and the most likely source of supply is from companies that manufacture such articles for jewellers.

The photograph (Illus. 12) shows you clasps and discs which are perforated so you can stitch the medallions to the metal. The perforated metal is called a screen or sieve. Screens for brooches (round and rectangular) come provided with a pin and catch and are known as "bar pin plaques." At the top of the photograph is a part for a cuff link. This has a hollow (concave) plate into which a bead or beadwork can be glued. Also, ear clips—flat, hollow, or perforated—are available for making earrings.

In cases where you cannot obtain the finding suggested for the project, you will have to either make your own finding or redesign the project slightly and use a substitute finding. For instance, if you cannot get a perforated clasp, you can wire the back of a perforated disc so it can be joined from the other side of the necklace by a "choker hook." Or you can substitute a "box clasp," and make a necklace without a medallion on the end. See Illus. 17, in the next project.

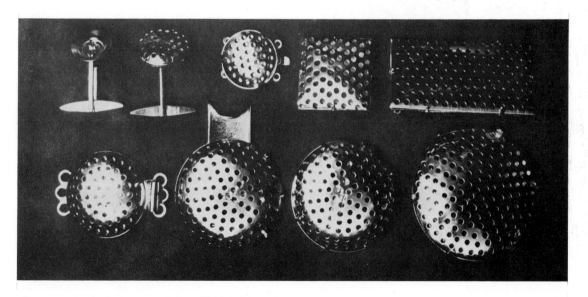

Illus. 12. Metal "findings" include cuff link holders, clasps and discs or rectangles to which beads can be glued or sewn.

Crystal Necklace

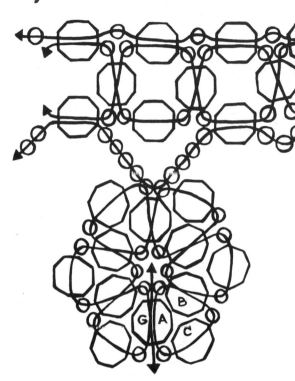

Illus. 13. Necklace is threaded in the basic technique with an additional thread on top and one on bottom to add small beads and medallions.

The necklace shown in Illus. 13 and 14 was threaded with crystal beads. Between the crystals, small, round glass beads were placed. Nylon fishing line was used for the threading, which was done according to the basic technique.

Notice you will need a metal clasp that has a tongue with eyelets (Illus. 15) and a screen to which you can attach a medallion (Illus. 16). (The tongue fits into the screened part of the clasp for opening and closing.)

First run a thread through two eyelets of the tongue in such a way that the thread-end emerging from the first eyelet and the thread-end emerging from the third eyelet have the same length. String two small beads through each thread-end, run both threads through a crystal bead so they cross and then continue in the basic technique (Illus. 15).

Illus. 13, 15 and 16 show that you thread one small glass bead between each crystal bead. Also, by making use of a separate thread tied to the first eyelet, you add small beads to the top of the necklace. Similarly, a separate thread tied to the bottom eyelet allows you to make little arches of beads at the lower side of the necklace and to attach the medallions (Illus. 13).

The medallions, all of the same size, are made without a central bead. Follow Illus. 13 for threading. Such a medallion is also attached to the screen of the clasp (Illus. 16). But for the clasp medallion, a small central bead is added last with

Illus. 14. Sparkling necklace consists of crystal beads with arches of small, round beads.

the inward-pointing thread, which is then glued into the crystal bead directly opposite.

Attaching the medallion to the screen must be done systematically, with neat stitches that do not pass *through* the beads, but instead pass over the threads of the medallion *between* the beads. In this project, before sewing the medallion on, cover the screen with white leather to hide the metal. (Use glue.)

After you finish threading, you attach the thread-ends to the other half of the clasp—the screen, which also has eyelets. Illus. 16 shows the four thread-ends leading to the screen, which is covered by the medallion. Knot the threads after they have been threaded through the eyelets of the screen. Then rethread the ends (with some glue applied) through a few beads and fix them.

This necklace is threaded in such a way that it stands somewhat against the neck, while the medallions lie flat. The materials used and the

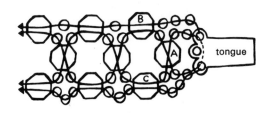

Illus. 15. Dotted line indicates the looped thread behind the tongue of the clasp where necklace begins.

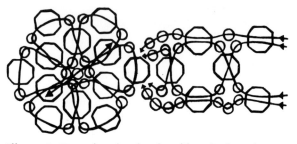

Illus. 16. Four thread-ends of necklace lead to the screen covered by the medallion.

15

design both make this necklace very suitable to wear with a low-cut dress. The medallions gracefully border the décolletage.

Of course, this design can be threaded with glossy colored beads as well. Such beads flatter by their glittering and can be worn at all ages. You can make matching earrings for this necklace by following the medallion design, but using slightly smaller beads. The medallions are attached to ear clips by either sewing them or glueing them on.

As mentioned on page 13, you can make your own sieved clasp if necessary. Fasten wire through perforations of a disc so that the wire forms a vertical bar down the back (Illus. 17). Adjust the tautness of the wire to allow room for a hook to close over it. Begin threading the hook (a "choker hook" with three eyelets) in the same way as you would for the tongue of a screened clasp. Continue with all the steps already described. In this case, however, the thread-ends of the finished necklace will have to be attached directly to the perforated disc, which has no eyelets attached. This means that the medallion is sewn on to the disc afterwards.

An alternative is to dispense with the medallion-decorated clasp altogether and use a simple "box clasp" (Illus. 17).

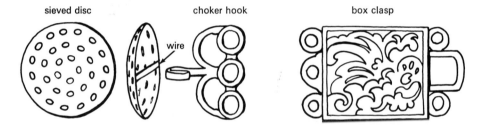

sieved disc   choker hook   box clasp

wire

Illus. 17. Make your own finding with a perforated disc, wired to be joined by a choker hook. Or substitute a box clasp for a medallion-decorated closure.

**Necklace
with Pendant
and Fringe**

Illus. 18. This necklace uses the basic technique plus extra threads for the fringe. The threading is diagrammed on the next page.

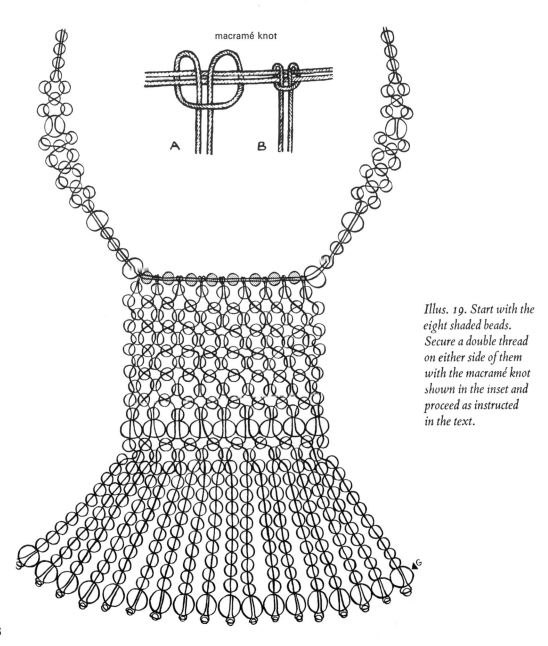

macramé knot

A   B

Illus. 19. Start with the eight shaded beads. Secure a double thread on either side of them with the macramé knot shown in the inset and proceed as instructed in the text.

Necklace with Pendant and Fringe

To make the necklace in Illus. 18 and 19, you first position eight beads in the middle of *two* threads of the intended length of the necklace. Then you tie the threads around something stationary so they are secured. In front of the first of the eight threaded beads (the shaded ones in Illus. 19), knot a separate long thread around the original two threads. Use the macramé knot shown in drawings A and B. This gives you two thread-ends of equal length.

In front of each bead, knot another separate thread in the same way and continue until after the eighth bead. Now, nine double threads hang from the original threads, which are being held in a fixed position. Next, thread a bead to each double thread, so that the first horizontal row of the pendant has nine beads. To continue, disregard the very first thread hanging down and the very last one, for the time being. (They will be used again when you thread both outer rows of the pendant.) This leaves 16 hanging threads which you work with in the basic technique to make the next nine horizontal rows. The horizontal rows consist alternately of nine and eight beads. Since the first row already has nine beads, the second will have eight. You end the basic technique with row 10, which also has eight beads.

For row 11, you thread nine beads in a simple straight way and you do the same with row 12, but you use larger beads. As you see in the drawing, the threads cross again in row 13, for which you use eight beads. This ends the pendant and the 16 threads are now used for threading the fringe. The two outer threads which were left out before are also used.

As you see in Illus. 19, each outer thread goes down a side of the pendant, and at every second row (beginning with row 2) an extra bead is threaded on to each side. Ultimately, each of these two outer threads passes through a large bead at the outside and then serves for threading the outsides of the fringe. The drawing clearly shows that at the bottom of the fringe, first a large bead is inserted and then, at the end, a small bead to finish. The part of the necklace that goes around your neck is threaded with the two original threads according to Illus. 19.

Necklace of Combined Threads

The necklace shown in Illus. 20 and 21 was executed in the basic technique, combined with a fringe. It was made of round red beads, cylindrical black-and-white beads and small silver beads. Such a necklace can also be threaded attractively with wooden beads.

Before you start threading, attach a double thread to each of two eyelets on one side of the clasp. (You can use the macramé knot for this.) Thread-ends from each double thread are used according to the basic technique, creating two separate series of strung beads, which are then joined as is clearly shown by Illus. 20. The upper series is made with round beads; the lower series consists of alternating round and cylindrical beads. Two threads attached to two eyelets are used to add small silver beads at the top of the necklace and the fringe at the bottom.

First you string the two series of beads in the basic technique. When they are long enough to drape themselves nicely around your neck, you attach the threads you used to the eyelets of the other part of the clasp. Rethread and glue the two ends into some beads.

The next stage is the threading together of both series of beads (Illus. 20). Therefore you take a new thread and place a round red bead (A) in the middle of that thread. With one end of that thread you now thread through a bead of the upper string and with the other end you thread

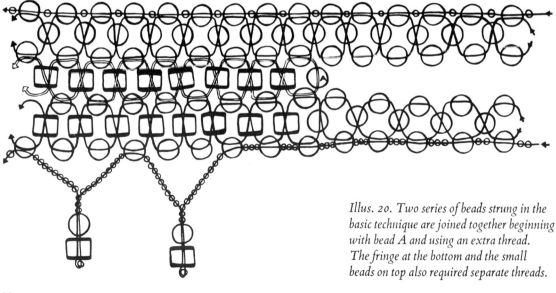

Illus. 20. Two series of beads strung in the basic technique are joined together beginning with bead A and using an extra thread. The fringe at the bottom and the small beads on top also required separate threads.

Illus. 21. The bayonet catch used with this necklace provides you with many eyelets for threading.

through a bead of the lower series. Now you insert a new bead, this time a cylindrical one, in which both threads cross. Then you thread both ends again, one through a bead of the upper string and the other through a bead of the lower string. After this, you again insert a new cylindrical bead, in which both threads cross—to be then threaded through a bead of the upper string and through a bead of the lower string. You repeat this until both strings have been threaded together over the length you desire. You end with a round red bead, like A, in which you fix the thread.

When the previous steps are finished you start with the fringe, strung with the thread attached to a bottom eyelet. Add the small silver beads between the large round ones and thread the fringe as shown in Illus. 20. Finally, at the top row of the necklace, thread small silver beads between the large ones, using the other extra thread at the top. This makes the necklace hang better.

If you study the photograph (Illus. 21) carefully, you will notice that a different type of clasp has been used for this necklace. In the trade it is known as a "bayonet catch." These catches exist in different sizes and with a different number of eyelets. More eyelets make it possible to thread necklaces which have a larger number of strings.

The finishing of a necklace—or other objects—must be done in a logical way to obtain good results. You always rethread in the direction from which the threads came. It is easy to understand why; only in this way can the suppleness of the threaded beads be maintained.

While the instructions for making this necklace may seem somewhat intricate, in practice, the execution will be less difficult than you may suppose. Of course, you should study the photograph and the drawing carefully before starting.

Jet Ornaments

Jet beads have been used for a long time in making ornaments. This has been proven by relics of the bronze age that have been found in Britain. Their glitter gives an air of gaiety and festivity. They are also suitable for persons of any age, and they are not subject to changes in fashion.

Jet is a hard black substance allied to coal. Ornaments made of jet should be confined to combining the beads only with other black material, like glass bars. Since color combinations are out of the question, a more refined design is generally used.

Illus. 22 shows a necklace with a bracelet and an earring. The ornaments have been made with jet beads combined with little bars and beads of black glass.

For the bracelet in the picture, you again apply the basic technique, using four beads (actually two beads and two bars). However, these are threaded with thin elastic of the type used for hats, or with rubber thread. If you use rubber thread, which is very thin, you must thread the beads twice or use a double thread. In making a bracelet, you should stretch the rubber thread a little to make the bracelet fit. As pointed out on page 8, you can easily make a necklace of jet beads and glass bars to match this bracelet.

Notice the purity in design of the necklace in the photograph. It has only one simple medallion attached. A diagram (Illus. 23), for making a similar medallion is given on the next page.

Illus. 22. Jet ornaments such as this necklace, earrings and bracelet must be simple in design. Jet should only be combined with other substances that are black.

You start the medallion with beads A, B and C and you continue as shown in the drawing. For a necklace, you can attach the medallion with a separate thread or you can attach it while threading the necklace.

This medallion design is also appropriate for a brooch. Before attaching it to the screen, you have to cover the screen by glueing on a small piece of black leather. This covering is necessary to prevent the metal of the screen from showing through the beads and ruining the effect. As mentioned before, the medallion must be sewn to the screen with neat stitches that pass over the threads of the medallion between the beads. Only in this way will the medallion retain its shape and stay in place.

For the small jet earrings, the beads and bars were attached separately to the screen of the ear clip, after the screen had been covered with some leather glued to it. The fringe consists of five parts (odd numbers always give a nicer effect) of varying lengths (see Illus. 24).

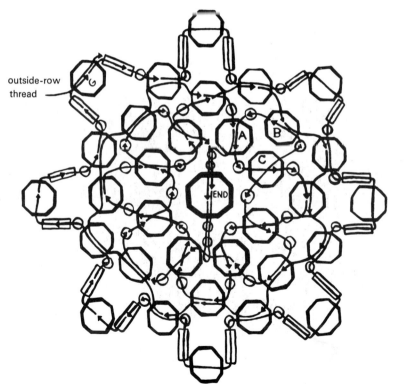

outside-row thread

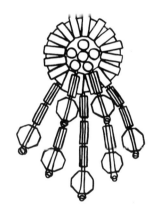

Illus. 23 (left). The basic thread in this medallion ends in point marked X. The outside row is threaded separately.

Illus. 24 (above). The fringe of this jet earring was added by sewing each thread-end separately to the screen.

Necklace and Earrings of Venetian Beads

Illus 25. The necklace of Venetian beads uses the basic technique combined with special threading for the fringe. This and the matching earring (below, left) are diagrammed on the next pages.

Necklace and Earrings of Venetian Beads

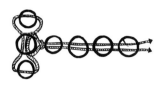

Illus. 26. Start with a three–bead clasp and attach necklace thread to middle bead. String seven or eight beads, then begin basic threading.

The necklace in Illus. 25 and 27 was made with the basic technique combined with a special threading. Also, instead of starting with a bar for the clasp, you begin with a row of three beads strung together as shown in Illus. 26. Attach your necklace thread to the middle bead and run both ends (of equal length) through seven single beads before continuing. Then use the basic technique

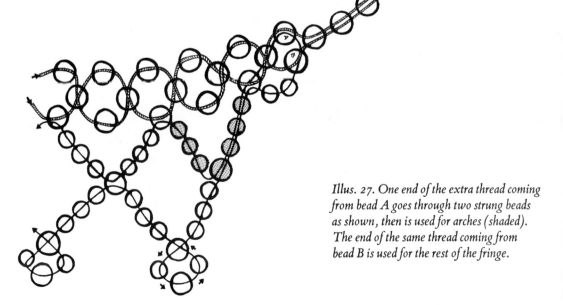

Illus. 27. One end of the extra thread coming from bead A goes through two strung beads as shown, then is used for arches (shaded). The end of the same thread coming from bead B is used for the rest of the fringe.

until you obtain the desired length—leaving room for the other half of the clasp. Thread four single beads and the beaded loop of the clasp at the end, and cut both threads off in the usual way.

Next, you again take a long thread, the middle of which you put between beads A and B. With the end emerging from bead A, you thread small arches of seven beads each. (The beads of the first arch are shaded in Illus. 27.) The end emerging from bead B you first use to thread two beads; after that you proceed as shown in Illus. 27.

Illus. 28 refers to the earring at the middle left of the color photograph on page 25. This ornament was threaded by using thin metal thread with glass bars and stone beads according to the basic technique. The method of threading is the same as that used for the red coral necklace on page 7, but in this case you do not put beads between the bars at the upper side, so that the bars enclose the large central bead in fanlike fashion.

The used thread is finished in the large bead and then you glue this bead to the ear clip. In this case, the so-called "hollow" clip is necessary.

Illus. 28. Thread the earring in the same way as the necklace on page 7, leaving out the top bead. Fanlike arrangement goes around central bead, where threads are finished.

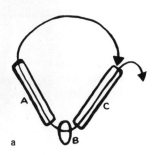

a

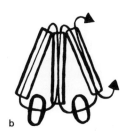

b

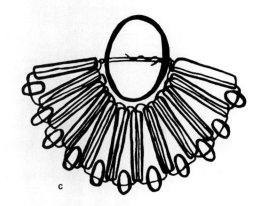

c

Earrings and Eardrops

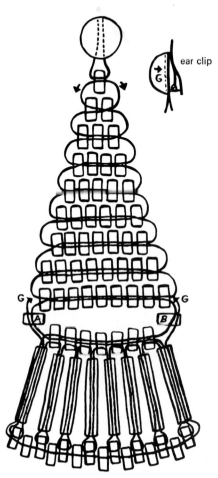

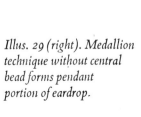

ear clip

Illus. 29 (right). Medallion technique without central bead forms pendant portion of eardrop.

Illus. 30. Thread from A goes through seven horizontal beads and through glass bars twice, adding bottom paillette. Thread from B goes through the same seven beads, through the outside left bar, through the paillettes, up the outside right bar and back into B.

In general, the medallion technique is applied for earrings made of beads. A small round medallion is made and sewn or glued to the screen of the ear clip, which has been covered by some thin leather to hide the metal. By adding a pendant, you can make an eardrop.

For the eardrop partially diagrammed in Illus. 29 (and pictured at the left on page 29), wooden beads were threaded according to the medallion technique, but without a central bead. Then one thread was beaded to form a string. This pendant was then attached to an ear clip covered by another medallion.

The eardrop diagrammed in Illus. 30 (and pictured on page 29) was made from paillettes— wooden beads in the shape of slices—combined with glass bars. Use the basic technique (starting with three beads) in such a way that each row has one more bead. After the final row, insert two horizontal beads and add the fringe, with the same threads, as shown. For this eardrop, you fix the threads to a flat clip and glue a halved wooden bead to it. To easily split a round wooden bead, put the bead with its opening on a thumb-tack to hold it in position. Then hold a sharp knife on the bead, tap the knife lightly with a hammer and the bead will split.

The diagrams on this page illustrate various other ways to make eardrops. In the first example, one thread is used for the medallion and the middle string of beads, while another thread is used for the outside strings. In the second example, the central bead is surrounded by the medallion technique, one end of the thread is cut off and the other serves to thread the fringe.

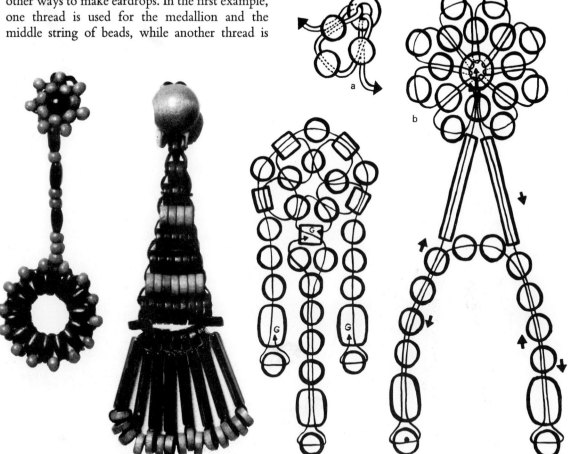

Illus. 31. The first two eardrops are diagrammed on the opposite page. Other ways of threading earrings are shown by the next two examples. Diagram labelled a is start of medallion for b.

Illus. 32. Pearls and crystal beads are used for this necklace. Matching eardrop is formed by matting technique discussed in next chapters.

Necklace and Eardrops with Pearls

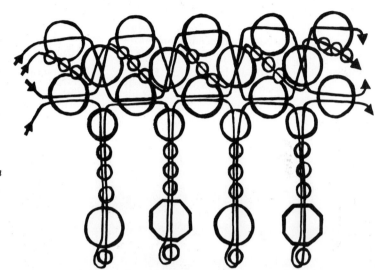

Illus. 33. Extra thread allows addition of small beads over basic pattern. Fringe also requires separate thread.

The necklace, part of which is shown at the top of the photograph on the opposite page, was threaded with pearl beads, combined with crystal beads and small round glass beads. All the steps are shown in Illus. 33.

To make this design, first thread the pearls by using the basic technique. With a separate thread inserted through the second row of pearls, add clusters of three glass beads threaded so that they are fixed diagonally over the pearls. This enlivens the necklace.

The fringe also requires a separate thread, which is run through the bottom row of pearls and through each string of beads that hangs from it. The strings of the fringe alternately end with a pearl and a crystal bead. The necklace is intended to stand against the neck, while the fringe lies flat.

The matching eardrop was made according to the matting technique, which you will learn about on the following pages. Fishing line was used for both ornaments. In this case, the beads which decorate the catch of the necklace and the clip of the eardrop were not first threaded in medallion forms, but were attached separately to the screen.

Matting Technique

Illus. 34 shows a hair ornament which has been decorated with beads in the matting technique. For this technique, you again need a long thread (depending on the size of the opening in the beads, a nylon fishing line or a plastic cord). Illus. 35 gives you step-by-step diagrams of how the threads cross each time, how the ornament can be widened at the end of the row to obtain a kind of "mat," and how a single row can be turned at the corner.

For the hair ornament, the beadwork was fixed to a rectangular screen, to which a hair clasp was attached. The ornament was executed in black and white stone beads. Other colors may be chosen, of course, but it is necessary that they contrast.

Illus. 36 pictures other objects which can be made with the matting technique, objects such as table mats, tumbler-holders and frames for a portrait or a mirror. The last drawing in Illus. 35 indicates the threading for such a frame. Special attention is needed at the corners in order to thread correctly.

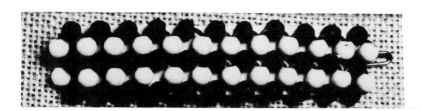

Illus. 34. The hair ornament at the left was made according to the matting technique.

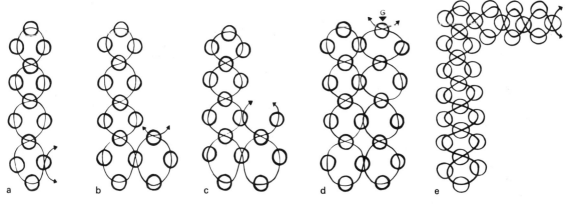

Illus. 35. Matting begins with basic threading but threads cross in side bead, allowing more beads to be strung. Step e shows how to turn a corner for making frame shapes.

Illus. 36. Matlike arrangement of beads is used for picture frames, tumbler-holders and table mats.

Necklace Using the Matting Technique

For necklaces, even though the beads are connected in a matlike fashion, the matting technique requires two threads instead of one. This is so that each row may be fastened securely to the clasp. The necklace in Illus. 37 (a diagram of the necklace on the cover) was made by applying the matting technique with a fringe added to the bottom and extra beads inserted at the top. The method followed is a combination of the techniques already used for the necklaces described on pages 14 and 20.

You start by pulling a thread through each of the three eyelets at one side of the clasp, forming twin threads of equal length. In this way, you have six threads to work with. With the top two threads, string a series of beads in the basic technique. Use the next two threads to string another series of beads in the basic technique, but use the bottom bead of the first series as one of your four beads. The last two threads go straight across, connecting the last-strung series with additional large and small beads.

Now you use a new thread, passing it through both the upper and lower eyelets, and positioning it so that both ends are equally long. With the upper end, you thread a small ring-shaped bead between each two beads at the top of the necklace. After this, you pull the thread taut to give the necklace its round collar-like shape. With the thread from the bottom eyelet, you add the fringe, threading the beads as shown in the drawing.

You will notice in the photograph on the cover that the necklace was threaded with a specially-made double catch consisting of two screens hooked together. Of course, a single catch—as used for the crystal necklace on page 15—can be used as well.

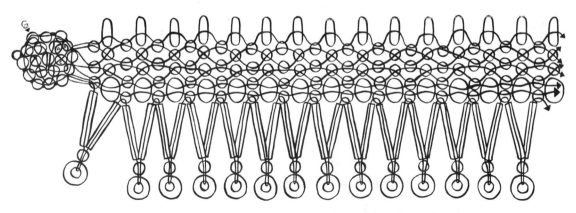

Illus. 37. The matting technique with more than one thread forms this necklace, featured on the cover.

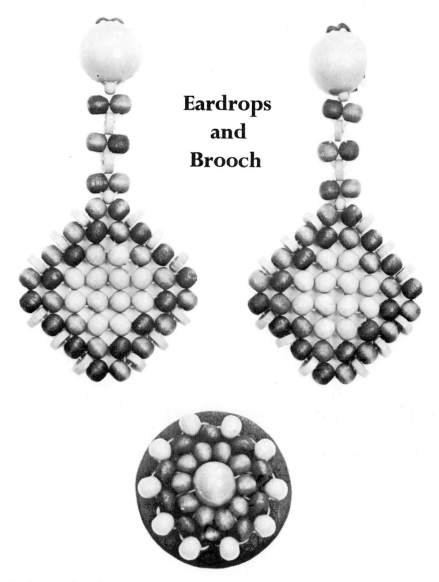

**Eardrops
and
Brooch**

Illus. 38. Eardrops made in the matting technique and a matching brooch are diagrammed on the next page.

Eardrops and Brooch

Illus. 39. Start where arrow points to numbered beads. Threads cross where two arrows face each other.

single arrow and the numbered beads. The threads cross at the lower point of the eardrop, and they then continue through the outer beads of the eardrop, where you use them to insert a "sliced" bead (a paillette) between each two beads. At the corners, however, no paillette is inserted.

At the upper point of the eardrop, you add a small bead in which the threads cross again. From there they continue upward to be fixed under the halved bead. On page 28, directions are given for halving a wooden bead.

The matching brooch (Illus. 38 and 40) was made of a medallion according to the instructions for Illus. 9. The medallion was then attached to a leather-covered screen of a brooch.

The eardrops of wooden beads in Illus. 38 were made with the matting technique. You can see in Illus. 39 where to start. This is indicated by the

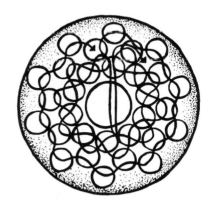

Illus. 40. Brooch is done in medallion technique, with upward-pointing thread going through outside row and inward-pointing thread used for the central bead.

Illus. 41. The colorful necklace begins with the matting technique and has fringes added as diagrammed on the next page. Above are two cloth-covered boxes that have been embroidered with beads. Such embroidery is explained in the chapter that follows.

Necklace of Bright Wooden Beads

The bright necklace which appears in color on the previous page was made of glossy wooden beads, threaded in the matting technique. It is fashioned in such a way that it forms a collar around the neck.

The necklace's upper, middle and bottom rows each has a fringe threaded between the beads. The fringes combine differently shaped wooden beads—round slices, oblong beads, triangular and four-sided beads.

Illus. 42 shows how the bottom fringe is threaded to the necklace. For the sake of clarity, only one row of fringe is diagrammed; actually there are three parallel rows, which gives a lively, playful effect. The color photograph on page 37 also shows a matching ring. For this, the beads were sewn directly to the screen instead of being formed into a medallion first. The same applies to the clasp of the necklace, decorated with the same beads.

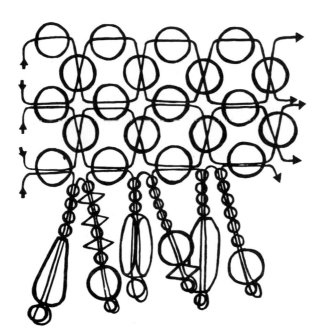

Illus. 42. Use a separate thread to add a fringe to the bottom row. The top row and the middle row also have a fringe strung by separate threads. The necklace is begun like the one on page 37, only with four thread-ends instead of six.

Embroidery with Beads

Illus. 43. Small beads applied to either felt (top two boxes) or leather (bottom boxes) result in ornate, useful items.

It is possible to apply the techniques described on the preceding pages to decorate a material (felt, silk, leather) with beads. Small beads must be used for this purpose. You can thread the beadwork separately and then sew it on to the material, or you can embroider the beads directly to the material. You can use bead embroidery to enhance clothes or articles such as little boxes for jewels, cigarettes, matches, cards, etc.

The color photograph on page 37 and the photograph here (Illus. 43) show several decorated little boxes, of which some have been covered with felt and others with thin leather (glove leather, lining leather).

Illus. 44. Embroidery with beads is a play with color and form. Circular and star-shaped designs are the most basic.

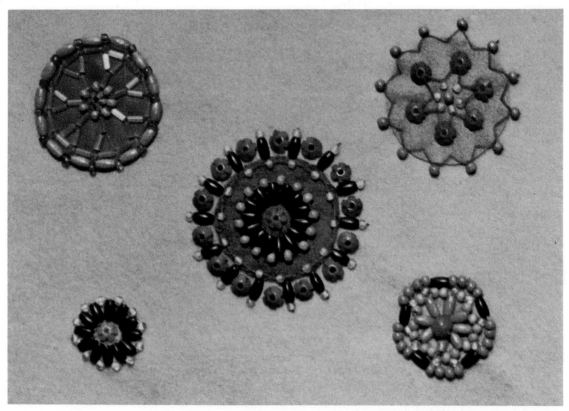

Illus. 45. Combining oval and round beads, small glass bars and rosette-shaped beads in different patterns give a wide range of possibilities.

Illus. 46. Examples of flat or sliced beads (center) are flanked by works employing them in designs.

To embroider a design of beads on your material, we suggest the following technique. First draw a circle (with French or tailor's chalk) on the material, making the circle the size you want the finished design to be. Then by drawing thin lines, divide the circle into eight equal parts. Begin the embroidery in the middle of the circle with a paillette or "sliced" bead and then continue from the middle radially towards the edge. Use the eight lines as a guide to placing eight main beads (the shaded ones in Illus. 47), around which you build your design. As you see in Illus. 47 and 48, many variations are possible.

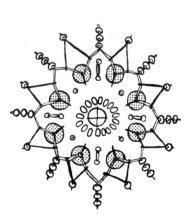 

Illus. 47. Eight main beads (shaded ones) are the basis around which you shape your further embroidery.

Illus. 48. Beads are held in place with any appropriate stitch. The "Y" stitch can be incorporated into design.

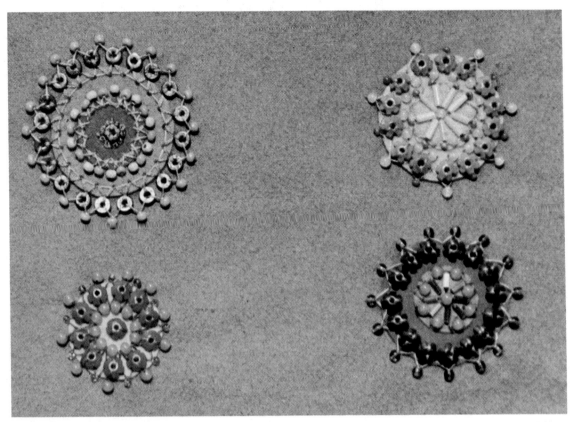

Illus. 49. Mixture of colors should be lively, whether subtle, as light blue and yellow, or vivid, as red and blue.

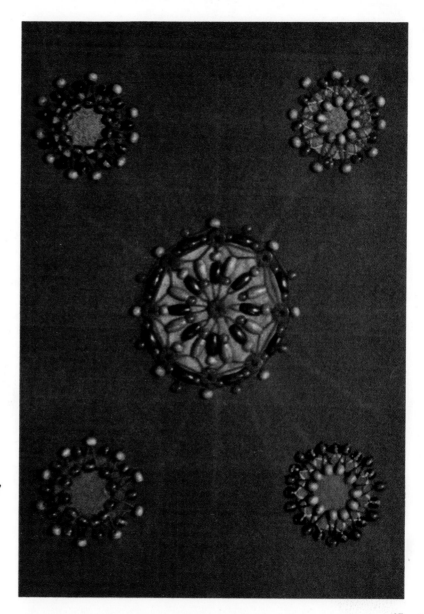

Illus. 50. Variety of pink and red beads are effectively united with each other and with green or yellow–orange beads.

You can sew separate beads on to the material with any stitch that seems appropriate. However, to secure beads to each other and keep them in the right place, you may find the chain stitch and variations of it (Illus. 51) very helpful.

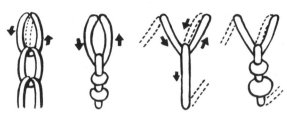

Illus. 51. Stitches: Chain stitch, chain with beads, Y stitch, Y with beads.

After the material has been decorated, it can be used for covering various articles—a box, for instance—by glueing it on. You should do this carefully and apply very little glue so it will not penetrate the material.

For finishing the edge of a piece of material (for instance the top of the box at the upper right side of Illus. 43), you use a buttonhole stitch with three beads threaded between each stitch (Illus. 52). It is also possible to attach two pieces of material together (the top and the side of the box in Illus. 43). You add a row of buttonhole stitches at the upper edge of the box's side, threading the stitches through the same beads already fixed to the rim (Illus. 53).

The color photographs on the preceding pages show other examples of embroidery with beads. Illus. 54 provides you with a variety of designs.

Another attractive use for embroidered material is to make a frame around a mirror. First, make a frame of thick cardboard in the desired size; then glue on a layer of thin foam rubber. Around this, glue the embroidered material. Such a frame can be made for a round as well as for a rectangular mirror.

Embroidery with beads has a long tradition which originated in the Far East. The ancient Egyptians, for example, decorated their plain linens with small pieces of leather in striking colors, finished with beads. The precious robes

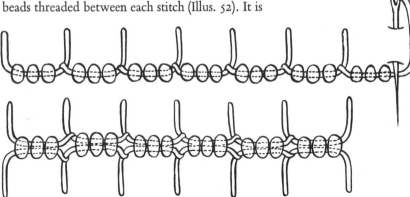

Illus. 52 (above). Plain buttonhole stitch with beads is used for finishing edges.

Illus. 53 (left). Another row of the same stitch added to sewn beads is used to join two edges of material.

Illus. 54. Here are five ideas for designs. Historical examples of bead embroidery can also inspire you.

used by the Church in the Middle Ages were embroidered with gold thread, precious stones and pearls; so was the splendid attire worn during the Renaissance in Italy and at royal courts in Spain, France and England.

Magnificent examples of embroidery with beads displayed in museums will inspire you. By copying the patterns you find in this book and elsewhere, you will train your eye and educate your taste. The more ideas you acquire by looking at the splendid objects from the past or from popular art, the more you will feel inclined to make something of beauty yourself.

In all the projects you create with beads, you will notice that the work gradually proceeds more and more smoothly. It is a play with beads and with colors. The results can be compared to a kaleidoscope. The movement of the color patterns in endless variations on the same theme is not only fascinating to look at, but is also very instructive and inspiring.

At the beginning, do not strive too high; it is not necessary and will only lead to discouragement. Only aim at playing with beads and color, and by doing so discover some of the joy of the creative artist.

Index

ACKNOWLEDGMENTS

The publishers wish to thank Colette Metz-la Croix for the beadwork on the cover and on pages 17 and 35, and Ingrid Valerie for the beadwork on pages 30 and 37.